Australia ABCs

A Book About the People and Places of Australia

Country ABCs

Written by Sarah Heiman
Illustrated by Arturo Avila

Australia Advisors:

Angelika Sauer, Ph.D.
Associate Professor of History and
Chair of the Department of History and Geography
Texas Lutheran University, Seguin, Texas

Markus Matthews, Ph.D.
Australasian Specialist and Citizen of Australia

Reading Advisor:

Lauren A. Liang, M.A.
Literacy Education, University of Minnesota
Minneapolis, Minnesota

PICTURE WINDOW BOOKS
Minneapolis, Minnesota

Many thanks to Brad Thompson, Australian citizen and husband of our content consultant
Dr. Angelika Sauer, for his firsthand knowledge of Australia and his insightful contributions to this book.

Editor: Peggy Henrikson
Designer: Nathan Gassman
Page production: Picture Window Books
The illustrations in this book were prepared digitally.

Picture Window Books
5115 Excelsior Boulevard
Suite 232
Minneapolis, MN 55416
1-877-845-8392
www.picturewindowbooks.com

Printed in the United States of America.
1 2 3 4 5 6 08 07 06 05 04 03

Library of Congress Cataloging-in-Publication Data
Heiman, Sarah, 1955–
Australia ABCs : a book about the people and places of Australia / written by Sarah Heiman ;
illustrated by Arturo Avila.
p. cm. — (Country ABCs)
Summary: An alphabetical exploration of the people, geography, animals, plants,
history, and culture of Australia. Includes bibliographical references and index.
ISBN 1-4048-0018-2 (lib. bdg. : alk. paper)
1. Australia—Juvenile literature. 2. Australia—Description and travel—Juvenile literature. 3. Australia—
Social life and customs—Juvenile literature. [1. Australia. 2. Alphabet.] I. Avila, Arturo, ill. II. Title. III. Series.
DU96 .H56 2003
994—dc21
2002006280

Australian words (a variation of English informally called "Strine") appear in *italics*.

G'day, mate!

This is how Australians greet each other. It means "Good day, friend." They call Australia "Oz" and themselves "Aussies" (OZZ-eez). Australia is an island country south of Asia. It is between the South Pacific Ocean and the Indian Ocean. About 19 million people live in Australia. It ranks 53rd in world population.

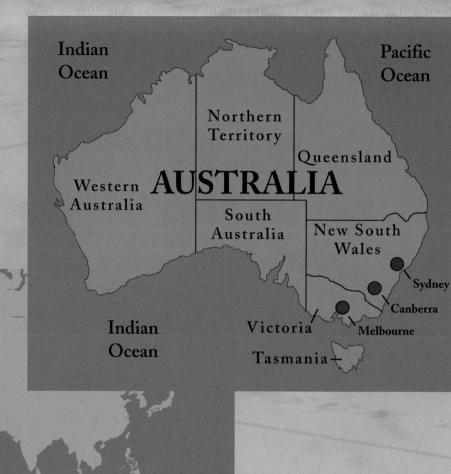

Australia is also called The Land Down Under, because it is under, or south of, the equator.

A is for Aborigine
(ab-uh-RIJ-uh-nee).

People have lived in Australia for at least 50,000 years. In the 1600s, explorers came from Europe. They called all the different peoples living there Aborigines. Aborigines still live in Australia today. Some paint their bodies for special ceremonies, but now they usually dress like other Australians.

Aborigines have names for their different groups. One name is the Koori. Other Aborigine groups are the Murri, Bama, Nunga, Wongi, Yolngu, Yuin, and Palawa.

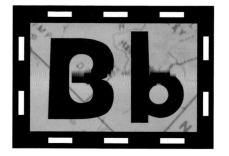

B is for boomerang.

A boomerang is a specially curved piece of wood. If you throw it with skill, it comes back to you. A boomerang is used for hunting and playing games. Ancient rock carvings in Australia show that people used boomerangs more than 14,000 years ago.

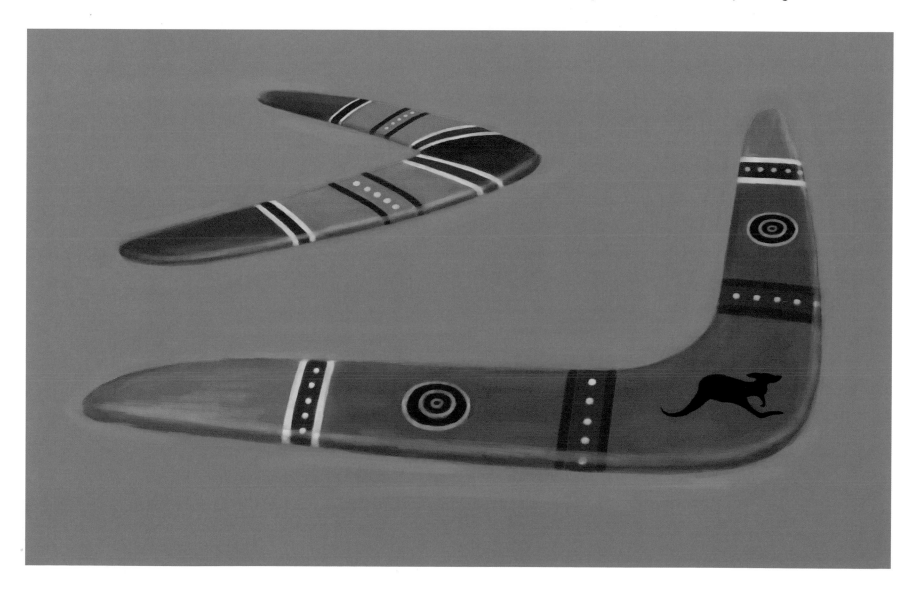

Cricket is a popular sport in Australia. It's played with a wide, flat bat and a hard, red ball that is slightly larger and heavier than a baseball. Games can last from one afternoon to five days! Cricket was brought to Australia from England.

C is for cricket.

D is for didgeridoo (did-juh-ree-DOO).

A didgeridoo is a musical instrument made from a tree branch that has been hollowed out by insects. Aborigines invented the didgeridoo long, long ago. They can make it sound like animal calls, a bubbling brook, or roaring thunder.

E is for eucalyptus
(yoo-kuh-LIP-tuss).

A eucalyptus tree, or "gumtree," has oily leaves with a strong smell. There are over 600 different kinds of eucalyptus trees. Koalas eat only eucalyptus leaves, which are poisonous to most other animals.

Australia's national flower is actually a flowering tree—the golden wattle.
September 1 is National Wattle Day. Everyone is encouraged to plant a tree or bush.

F is for flag.

Australia's flag shows Britain's flag in the upper-left corner. The large star on the flag stands for the six states and two territories of Australia. The small stars stand for the Southern Cross, a group of stars you can see when you are south of the equator.

Australia, like the United States, used to be several British colonies, or groups of people governed by Britain. In 1901, Australia became a country with its own government. Now it belongs to a group of nations led by Britain.

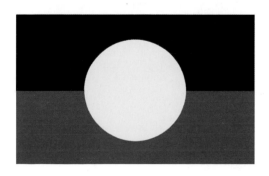

Aborigines have their own flag, plus the Australian flag. On the Aboriginal flag, the color black is for the people. Yellow stands for the sun, and red is for the earth.

G is for Great Barrier Reef.

The Great Barrier Reef is the world's largest coral reef. Coral are tiny, brightly colored sea creatures. The reef is made of both live coral and skeletons of dead coral. It is home to many beautiful fish and sea plants. The reef is so big, it can be seen from space.

H is for Harbour Bridge.

Tour groups can climb stairs to the top of the Harbour Bridge in Sydney. The climbers have to be tied to a safety rail as they climb. Their reward at the top is a great view of the city and Sydney Harbour.

The bridge spans 1,650 feet (503 meters) and carries up to 15,000 cars at a time.
It has eight car lanes, two train lines, a walkway, and a bike lane.

I is for island.

Australia is the largest island in the world. It is both a country and a continent. Most of the people live in large cities along the eastern seacoast. Tasmania, an island south of Australia, is Australia's smallest state. Aussies call Tasmania "Tassie" (TAZZ-ee).

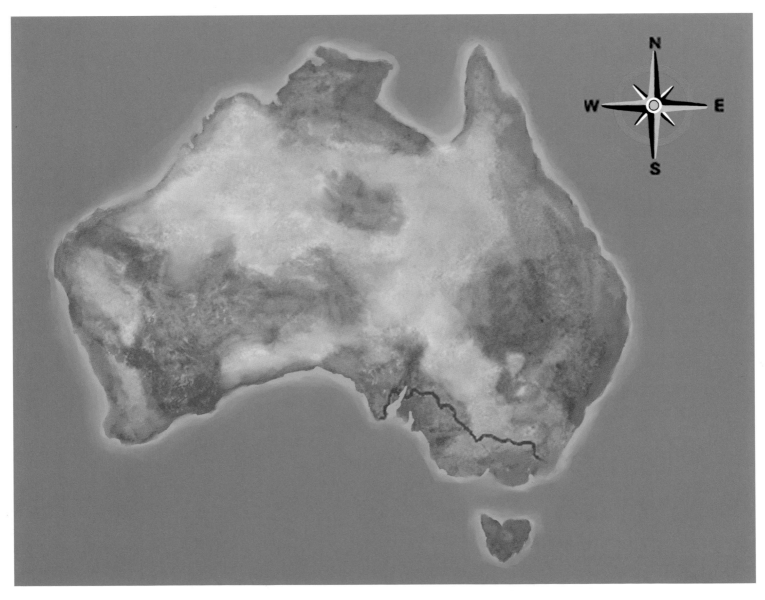

J is for *jackaroos* and *jillaroos*.

Australian cattle and sheep ranches are called stations.

New ranch workers, or stationhands, are called *jackaroos* and *jillaroos*.

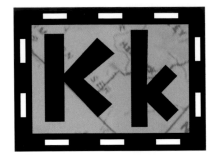

K is for kangaroo.

Kangaroos are a popular tourist attraction in Australia. A kangaroo is a marsupial, which is a mammal that raises its young in a pouch on its body. A baby kangaroo is called a joey.

Australia is home to many animals such as the kangaroo that don't live anywhere else in the world, except perhaps in zoos.

L is for lyrebird.

The Australian lyrebird gets its name from its amazing tail. The male's tail feathers spread out to form the shape of a lyre, an instrument that is like a harp. Lyrebirds can copy the calls of other birds and animals.

Lyrebirds can even copy sounds such as ringing phones and honking horns.

M is for money.

Australia's unit of money is the Australian dollar.

Australian money includes coins and bills.

The bills are printed on thin plastic instead of paper.

Queen Elizabeth II is pictured on the Australian five-dollar bill. She is the queen of Britain and also the queen of Australia. Since Australia became its own country in 1901, the queen is no longer as involved in the government there. Australians elect their own people to run their government.

N is for Nambung National Park.

The Nambung National Park in Western Australia is one of more than 500 national parks in the country. In Nambung, visitors can hike into the Pinnacles Desert, which has thousands of giant rock pillars jutting out of the yellow sand.

O is for Outback.

Beyond the coastal cities of Australia is a huge area known as the Outback. There are very few towns in the Outback. Most of it is desert. The rest of this land is grassland used for raising cattle and sheep. The Outback is also called the bush.

The largest sheep station in the Outback has about 70,000 sheep. Australia has nine times more sheep than people.

P is for platypus.

The platypus is one of only three mammals in the world that lay eggs. A platypus has a tail like a beaver's and a bill like a duck's. Platypuses live near rivers and lakes, and they live only in Australia.

Q is for Queensland.

Queensland is where many Aussies vacation, or go "on holiday." The state is famous for its beaches, tropical islands, lush rain forests, and the Great Barrier Reef.

Queensland

Queensland began as a colony of British prisoners in 1824. By the 1840s, other people were moving in. Today the state produces huge quantities of pineapples, bananas, mangoes, and sugarcane.

R is for radio.

In the Outback, children listen and talk to their teachers over the radio. The children live too far from any town to attend school. Students receive and send tests and homework through the mail. These days, they might use the phone, the Internet, and videos as well as the radio.

Australian children attend school from ages 5 to 15. Many keep going to school and eventually attend universities. Most schools give students a summer vacation in January. When it is winter in North America, it is summer in Australia.

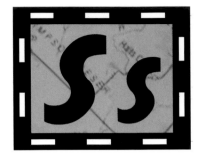

S is for Sydney.

Sydney is Australia's largest city. Like most Australians, many of Sydney's four million people come from other countries. Sydney is on the east coast of Australia and has over 40 beaches. It also has one of the most famous buildings in the world, the Sydney Opera House.

Both Sydney and Melbourne, Australia's two largest cities, wanted to be the capital. So the city of Canberra was built between the two, and it became the capital.

Sydney Opera House

T is for *tucker.*

Tucker is the Aussie word for food. Australian food is a blend of different countries' cooking styles. Aussies eat lots of fish and shellfish, and meat cooked on the *barbie* (barbecue). A small beef pie, often served with "sauce" (ketchup), is a favorite snack—especially while watching *footy,* or Australian football.

Other Aussie Foods

- *lamingtons*: small, square cakes, dipped in chocolate, and rolled in coconut
- Vegemite: a dark brown spread that comes from yeast and is used on toast and sandwiches
- *bush tucker*: foods found in the wild, such as berries, fruits, and insects as well as kangaroos, crocodiles, and birds. Aborigines lived on *bush tucker* for thousands of years.

U is for Uluru (oo-LOO-roo).

In the middle of Australia, a huge red rock rises from the flat earth. It is almost as tall as the Empire State Building. This sandstone rock is known as Uluru, or Ayers Rock. As the sun sets in the Outback, the rock seems to glow. Uluru is Australia's most popular tourist attraction.

Uluru is the ancient Aboriginal name for this rock, which is sacred to the Anangu Aborigines. The Aborigines call their religion the Dreaming. Most Australians are Christians. Other religions that people practice in Australia, besides the Dreaming, are Judaism, Islam, and Buddhism.

V is for Victoria.

Victoria is a state in southeastern Australia called the Garden State. Farmers in Victoria grow vegetables, apples, and grapes. Ranchers raise cattle for meat and sheep for meat and wool. The city of Melbourne is the capital of Victoria. Many of Australia's factories are in Melbourne.

Victoria is named for Queen Victoria. She ruled Britain—and the Australian colonies—from 1837 to 1901.

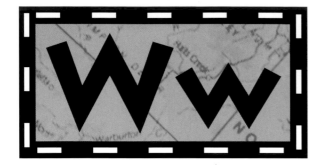

W is for "Waltzing Matilda."

Most Australians consider "Waltzing Matilda" to be the national song. It was written by Australian musician Andrew Barton ("Banjo") Paterson in 1895. The words "waltzing Matilda" mean traveling from place to place in search of work, carrying your belongings on your back.

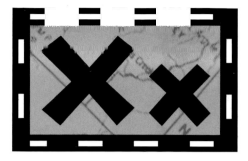

X is for eXports.

Australia exports more wool than any other country in the world and much of the world's wheat. The country also exports minerals such as coal, gold, and iron ore.

Y is for yabby.

A yabby is a freshwater crayfish. Yabbies look like small lobsters. They are a favorite Australian food. Catching yabbies is a popular pastime.

Z is for ANZAC Day.

ANZAC Day is named for soldiers of the Australian and New Zealand Army Corps (ANZAC) who fought in World War I. ANZAC Day is a national holiday on April 25, honoring people who have died in all wars. Children like to be in ANZAC Day parades.

Other Australian Holidays

• Australia Day (January 26) honors the day when the British first came to Australia.

• May 27 is a day to honor the Aboriginal peoples and apologize for how they were treated in the past.

• Queen's Birthday is celebrated in June.

• Boxing Day (December 26) is a day to relax after Christmas and give presents (in boxes) to people who work for you.

Aussie soldiers are called diggers.

Make Your Own Rock Paintings

Aborigines used rock paintings to keep a record of their lives.
Some Australian rock paintings and carvings are 30,000 years old!

What You Need

Rocks
Newspapers
Paint
A paintbrush

What to Do

1. Find some clean, flat rocks or stones.

2. Spread the newspapers down to protect your work area from paint.

3. Paint designs, patterns, or pictures on your rocks. You might draw things you see in nature.

4. Let the rocks dry.

5. Admire your creations!

A Taste of Strine

Aussies mostly speak English, but with their own accent and special words.
They call this variety of English "Strine." The name comes from the way
they pronounce *Australian* ("Au-STRINE").

barbie	barbecue	*lollies*	candy
chook	chicken	*bikkies*	cookies
mozzie	mosquito	*roo*	kangaroo
brekkie	breakfast	*mob*	family of *roos*

rain

rainbow, cloud, or cliff

footprints

star

sitting-down place

Fast Facts

Official name:	Commonwealth of Australia
Capital:	Canberra
Official language:	English
Population:	19,357,594
Area:	2,967,893 square miles (7,686,843 square kilometers)
Highest point:	Mount Kosciusko, 7,310 feet (2,228 meters)
Lowest point:	Lake Eyre, 52 feet (16 meters) below sea level
Type of government:	constitutional monarchy
Head of state:	British monarch (represented by an Australian governor general)
Head of government:	prime minister
Major industries:	mining, food processing, chemicals, steel, tourism
Natural resources:	coal, iron ore, gold, tin, zinc
Major agricultural products:	wheat, barley, cattle, sheep
Chief exports:	coal, meat, wool, alumina, iron ore, wheat
National animals:	kangaroo, emu (large, flightless bird)
National gemstone:	opal

Fun Facts

• Most Australian children spend their free time at the beach. They surf, snorkel, sail, and swim.
  Many join surf lifesaving clubs and become volunteer surf lifesavers when they get older.

• In the Outback, supplies arrive by "road train." These monster-size trucks are as long as trains.

• Australia is the world's largest producer of diamonds, but the opal is Australia's national gemstone.
  An opal may contain many different colors. An Aboriginal legend says a rainbow fell to Earth to create the opal.

• At the Hyde Park Barracks Museum in Sydney, Australians can type their names into a computer to find out if
  their ancestors were prisoners. (See page 20 for the history of prisoners in Australia.)

• The longest fence in the world is in Australia. The Dingo Fence is 3,700 miles (5,953 kilometers) long.
  It was built to keep wild dogs, or dingoes, from killing sheep.

Glossary

Aborigines (ab-uh-RIJ-uh-nees)—the name for all the native groups of people of Australia

bush (bush)—the large, wild areas of Australia where few people live; also known as the Outback

colony (KOL-uh-nee)—a group of people who leave their country and settle in a new land and who are governed by the country they came from. Both America and Australia started out as colonies governed by Britain.

didgeridoo (did-juh-ree-DOO)—a musical instrument made from a tree branch that has been hollowed out by insects

equator (i-KWAY-tur)—an imaginary line around the middle of the Earth. It divides the northern hemisphere (half of the Earth) from the southern hemisphere.

marsupial (mar-SOO-pee-uhl)—a mammal that raises its young in a pouch on its body

monarch (MON-ark)—someone who rules over a kingdom, such as a king or queen

Strine (STRINE)—a variation of the English language spoken by Australians

To Learn More

At the Library

Arnold, Caroline. *Australian Animals*. New York: HarperCollins, 2000.
Bagley, Katie. *Australia*. Mankato, Minn.: Bridgestone Books, 2003.
Gray, Shirley W. *Australia*. Minneapolis: Compass Point Books, 2001.
Grupper, Jonathan. *Destination: Australia*. Washington, D.C.: National Geographic Society, 2000.

On the Web

Embassy of Australia
http://austemb.org
Information about Australia, including a kids' page

CIA—The World Factbook (Australia)
http://www.cia.gov/cia/publications/factbook/geos/as.html
Facts about Australia from the U.S. Central Intelligence Agency

Want to learn more about Australia? Visit FACT HOUND at *http://www.facthound.com*.

Index